Signals from Space

The Chandra X-ray Observatory

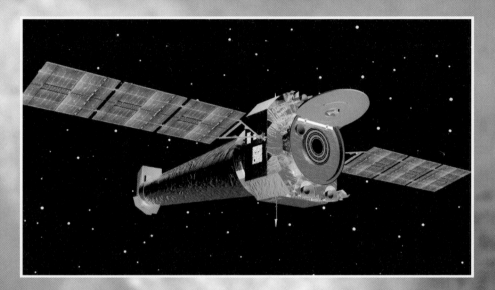

Robert Naeye

RAINTREE
STECK-VAUGHN
PUBLISHERS

A Harcourt Company

Austin · New York
www.steck-vaughn.com

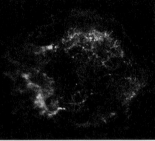

To the thousands of people whose hard work and skill made the dream of AXAF become the reality of Chandra.

Steck-Vaughn Company

First published 2001 by Raintree Steck-Vaughn Publishers, an imprint of Steck-Vaughn Company.

Copyright © 2001 Turnstone Publishing Group, Inc.
Copyright © 2001, text, by Robert Naeye.

Library of Congress Cataloging-in-Publication Data

Naeye, Robert.
      Signals from space: the Chandra X-ray observatory/Robert Naeye.
         p. cm. – (Space explorer)
      Includes bibliographical references and index.
      ISBN 0-7398-2215-2 (hardcover)
      ISBN 0-7398-2225-X (softcover)
      1. X-ray astronomy—Juvenile literature. 2. Astronautics in astronomy—Juvenile literature. 3. Chandra X-ray Observatory (U.S.)—Juvenile literature. [1. X-ray astronomy. 2. Chandra X-ray Observatory (U.S.) 3. Astronomy.] I. Title. II. Series.

QB472.5 .N342001
522'.6863—dc21   00-042452

For information about this and other Turnstone reference books and educational materials, visit Turnstone Publishing Group on the World Wide Web at http://www.turnstonepub.com.

Photo credits listed on page 64 constitute part of this copyright page.

Printed and bound in the United States of America.

1 2 3 4 5 6 7 8 9 0 LB 05 04 03 02 01 00

CONTENTS

X-RAYS FROM SPACE

"It was one of the most energetic things that we had seen in the universe and we had no idea what it could be."—Riccardo Giacconi

It was a warm, clear evening at the White Sands Air Force Base in the New Mexico desert. Just before midnight on June 18, 1962, a scientific team nervously watched a five-story-high rocket soar into the sky. The team hoped this rocket would pick up X-rays from space. X-rays are a kind of light that we can't see with our eyes.

Using rockets to try to detect X-rays from beyond our solar system was first suggested by scientist Bruno Rossi of the Massachusetts Institute of Technology. Bruno brought his idea to the American Science and Engineering Company (AS&E). AS&E formed a team, including Bruno and scientists Riccardo Giacconi, Frank Piolini, and Herbert Gursky, to test the idea.

The team in New Mexico had good reasons to be nervous. Two past rocket launches had failed. The first rocket had exploded. A doorway in the second rocket's nose cone, or front section, had failed to open.

Why did they keep launching rockets? Why couldn't they just build an X-ray telescope on the ground? It would be cheaper. If something broke, it would be easier to fix. The problem is that X-rays from outer space can't make it all the way to the ground. They are absorbed by some of the gases that make up Earth's atmosphere.

Five minutes into this flight, the team knew the launch was successful. In the rocket, devices called detectors started picking up X-rays from deep space.

(above)
This photograph shows the place in the sky where the rockets launched by the team found X-rays. The X-rays came from the circled part of the sky seen in the constellation Scorpius. A constellation is a set of stars that forms a recognizable pattern in people's imaginations.

(left)
The team of scientists used an Aerobee rocket like this one for their experiment.

5

Looking at the Universe

For a long time, scientists had been able to use only visible light to study the universe. Visible light is the kind of light we can see with our eyes. But a scientist who uses only visible light to look at the night sky is like an alien who listens to one country music radio station to learn about human music on Earth. Without hearing classical music, jazz, rock, and blues, the alien wouldn't have enough information to understand our music very well. Not long ago, scientists didn't have enough information to begin to understand the universe, either.

Then, in the mid-1900s, scientists first learned to build devices that could detect light that is invisible to human eyes. These devices opened new windows to the universe.

In 1948 scientists from the United States placed devices sensitive to X-rays on a German-designed rocket. Those devices picked up X-rays from space. But at that time, scientists could not tell where the X-rays were coming from. Then, in 1949, a team led by Herbert Friedman at the Naval Research Laboratory in Washington, D.C., conducted another rocket experiment. That experiment showed X-rays coming from the sun.

The team from AS&E expected to find X-rays from the sun near the moon, but they also looked toward the center of our galaxy. Surprisingly, the rocket picked up a

X-ray Vision

This picture, made in 1898, was one of the first X-ray images. It is an image of the Russian ruler Czarina Alexandra's lower arm, including her jewelry. To make this image, a machine produced X-ray light. Film that was placed behind the czarina's hand detected the X-ray light. The film does the same thing as X-ray detectors do in rockets.

Medical X-rays show density, or the amount of matter in a particular amount of space. In this X-ray, the bones and jewelry can be "seen" because they are dense and absorb X-rays. The film is unexposed, or dark, where X-rays are absorbed. The czarina's rings and bracelets, which are made of denser material than the bones of her hand, show the most clearly. Less dense objects, such as a person's skin, are transparent to X-rays. The X-rays pass through skin to the film, turning the film white.

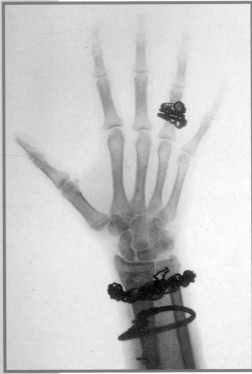

flood of X-rays from a small patch of sky in the constellation Scorpius. The team had discovered the first X-rays from outside our solar system. They named the new X-ray source Scorpius X-1.

An Important Discovery

X-rays can be produced by very hot objects and violent processes, such as the explosion of a star. The team's discovery of so many X-rays from one place was the first hint that there might be more of these violent processes in outer space than scientists had thought.

After discovering Scorpius X-1, the team looked at photographs taken in visible light of the same part of the sky. To their surprise, the visible light photographs didn't show any bright object at Scorpius X-1's position. Scorpius X-1 was producing more than 100 million times more X-rays than the sun, but Scorpius X-1 could not be seen in visible light. Some unusual process was clearly taking place in Scorpius X-1. "We had no idea what it could be," Riccardo recalls.

Scientists couldn't identify what was producing the X-rays that were coming from Scorpius X-1. But the team had discovered a distant source of X-rays. Many scientists had thought that nothing beyond our solar system could produce X-rays that could be detected from just above Earth's atmosphere. Finding Scorpius X-1 proved that this thought was wrong.

Here (from left to right), Riccardo Giacconi, Herb Gursky, and Fred Hendel examine the data obtained by one of the rockets. The data helped them determine from what direction the X-rays might be coming.

Visible and Invisible

Light is very mysterious. The more scientists study it, the more mysterious it seems. But some of its properties can be modeled fairly easily.

One property of light is the way it moves. Light often seems to travel in straight lines. When scientists first created a model of light, they used "rays" to represent this straight path.

Other properties of light require more complicated models. In the "wave" model, light is represented as waves of all different lengths. The light we see is called visible light. This light has a certain range of wavelengths. In a rainbow, different colors of light appear. They appear in this order—red, orange, yellow, green, blue, indigo, violet. In the wave model, wavelengths representing the colors of light become shorter in this same order. Red light has the longest wavelengths and violet light has the shortest wavelengths.

Light also sometimes behaves as if it were made of particles. In the particle model of light, each particle has a characteristic amount of energy. For example, a particle of X-ray light has much more energy than a particle of visible light.

Scientists have modeled light as rays, waves, and particles. But it's important to remember that these are only models.

This is one of the detectors that was carried in the rockets used by the team from AS&E. It is able to detect X-ray light.

Wave Model of Light

In the wave model of light, wavelengths can be from near zero to near infinity. Different objects and processes in nature give off different amounts of light at the various wavelengths.

According to the wave model, some objects give off light with long wavelengths, called radio waves. Other objects, like the human body, produce light called infrared. It has shorter wavelengths than radio waves. The universe's hottest processes give off mostly X-rays or gamma rays. These kinds of light have the shortest wavelengths.

The chart below shows names used for light of different wavelengths. Light with the shortest wavelengths is called gamma rays. Light with the longest wavelengths is called radio waves.

Because the Anglo-Australian Telescope (above) detects visible light, it can be located on Earth's surface. The picture at left of the Orion Nebula was taken by this telescope.

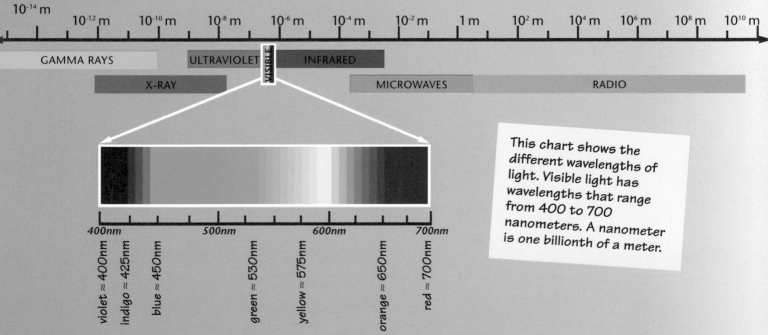

10^{-14} m 10^{-12} m 10^{-10} m 10^{-8} m 10^{-6} m 10^{-4} m 10^{-2} m 1 m 10^{2} m 10^{4} m 10^{6} m 10^{8} m 10^{10} m

GAMMA RAYS ULTRAVIOLET INFRARED VISIBLE

X-RAY MICROWAVES RADIO

400nm 500nm 600nm 700nm

violet ≈ 400nm indigo ≈ 425nm blue ≈ 450nm green ≈ 530nm yellow ≈ 575nm orange ≈ 650nm red ≈ 700nm

This chart shows the different wavelengths of light. Visible light has wavelengths that range from 400 to 700 nanometers. A nanometer is one billionth of a meter.

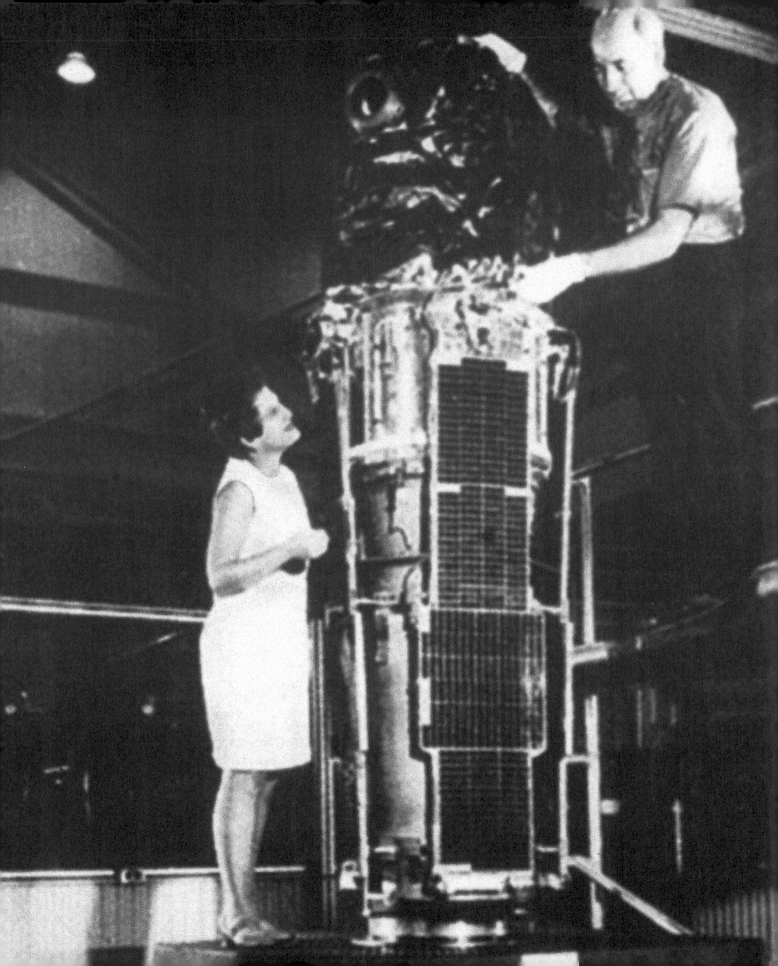

2

FLYING HIGH

"All of X-ray astronomy for the first decade was...about an hour of observation all together."—Riccardo Giacconi

After the discovery of Scorpius X-1, scientists were eager to learn more about the X-ray universe. During the 1960s, scientists launched more and more rockets. Using the rockets, scientists found about 30 X-ray sources outside our solar system.

But there was a limit to how much rockets could do. Usually rockets go up and come right back down in a matter of minutes. Scientists realized they needed an X-ray satellite. Unlike rockets, satellites go around Earth over and over again in a path called an orbit. A satellite can operate in space for months or years.

On December 12, 1970, a team including Bruno, Riccardo, and scientists and technicians from the National Aeronautics and Space Administration (NASA) launched a satellite. Its detector was about the size of a microwave oven. The satellite was launched from a platform in the Indian Ocean just off the coast of Kenya. The date was the seventh anniversary of Kenya's independence from Great Britain, so the team named the satellite Uhuru, the Swahili word for freedom.

Uhuru was a major success. It discovered 339 new X-ray sources. It also created a new puzzle for scientists.

(above)
The Uhuru satellite held only detectors. It didn't have a telescope. Because it could stay in orbit for a very long time, it could collect much more information than a rocket.

(left)
Scientists Marjorie Townsend, who gave Uhuru its name, and Bruno Rossi check the satellite before it is launched.

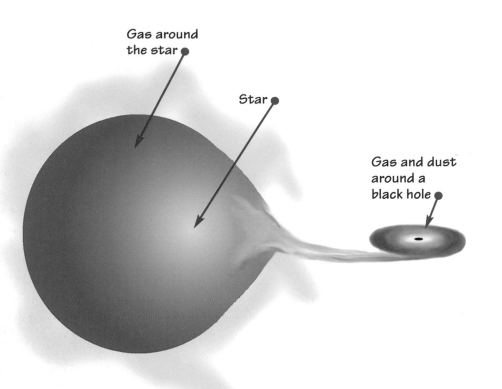

Gas around the star

Star

Gas and dust around a black hole

Giving Off X-rays

In scientists' models of black holes, X-rays come from hot gas from a nearby star. The gas moves from the star toward the black hole, moving like a whirlpool. Small particles in the gas bump into one another at speeds of hundreds of millions of kilometers per hour. This very hot gas gives off X-rays.

Above is an artist's picture of what a region around a black hole like Cygnus X-1 might look like. Gas and dust leave the star on the left. On the right, the gas and dust whirl around a black hole. The black hole itself can't be seen.

The amount of X-rays given off by many of these new sources changed over time. For some sources, these changes in strength happened quickly. What caused the changes?

One of the most powerful of these sources was Cygnus X-1, in the constellation Cygnus. Scientists used optical telescopes, the kind of telescopes that collect visible light, to study Cygnus X-1. Slowly they realized what Uhuru might have found. It seemed that Cygnus X-1 might be a black hole.

The great scientist Albert Einstein suggested a model that allowed other scientists to predict the possibility of black holes. Einstein's model shows how masses, or bits of matter, affect one another. Using this model and information from observations, scientists have developed other models of how black holes might form.

In the models, when a large star is at the end of its life, the material in its inner parts cools and falls in on itself. It gathers into a denser and denser mass. When the material is packed into a small enough space, nothing, not even light, can escape. For that reason, scientists call this kind of object a black hole.

Before Uhuru, scientists thought black holes existed, but they didn't have proof. "Cygnus X-1 was the first evidence found that black holes actually exist in nature," Riccardo says.

Making a Model

No one has ever seen a black hole. So how do scientists study them? To answer questions like these, scientists develop models. These models are guided by scientists' observations and by mathematical models of the "laws of physics."

The laws of physics are not really laws. People can't create a rule and expect nature to follow it. The laws of physics are models based on observations of nature's behavior. We call some models "laws" when nature seems to always behave in ways that these laws predict. These laws seem to hold true everywhere on Earth and also everywhere else in the universe.

All models are built from observations, so scientists must decide which model or models represent a process best. Because some models make predictions about processes that haven't been observed well, or even at all, new information can lead to a change in a model or make the creation of a new model necessary.

1 Collect Evidence

Scientists observe how nature behaves. They use rockets and satellites to gather information about objects in space, such as Cygnus X-1.

2 Use Scientific Models

Scientists think of conditions in nature that could lead to what they observe. They use these conditions and their models of how nature behaves to try to predict what might happen around a black hole.

3 Program Computers

These models are very complicated and require many calculations. So scientists use computers to make detailed predictions of the activity they might observe around a black hole. A model is useful if what it predicts agrees with the observations that scientists then make.

Solving X-ray Mysteries

When a large star explodes, the event is called a supernova. A supernova produces either a black hole or a very hot object called a neutron star. A neutron star is made almost entirely of neutrons. A neutron is an elementary particle, like a proton. But a neutron has no electrical charge. It is electrically neutral.

Models tell scientists that a supernova sends a star's outer layers into space. The inner parts fall in on themselves, creating a neutron star. In a neutron star, an enormous amount of matter fills a very small space. But the material in a neutron star is not so densly packed as in a black hole. A neutron star's diameter is about the same size as the width of a small city— about ten kilometers (about six miles). It is as if a giant trash compactor has squeezed the star. The material is so compact that one thimbleful of a neutron star has more matter than there is in 10 million elephants. But its matter is not so densely packed as it is in a black hole.

One model tells scientists that gas from a nearby star can crash into a neutron star. This can happen when the stars are so close that they orbit one another. The gas moves faster and faster as it comes closer to the star. It hits the star at high enough speed that X-rays are given off. Scientists' observations of the area near Scorpius X-1 agree with this model. Scientists therefore believe that this first discovery of an X-ray source in space is a neutron star. An X-ray mystery has probably been solved.

Scientists who study X-rays are interested in more than black holes and neutron stars. A star's death also has other results. When hot gas from a supernova slams

A supernova is so powerful that for a few days, one supernova can outshine an entire galaxy of billions of individual stars. Supernovae can create clouds of gas called supernova remnants. A remnant is something that is left over. Above is a picture of the Veil Nebula taken in visible light. It is the 30,000-year-old remnant of a supernova explosion.

into the gas that surrounded the star before it exploded, X-rays are given off. And when stars die, their outer layers hurtle outward into space. This material forms clouds of expanding gas called supernova remnants. Like the regions near black holes and neutron stars, remnants give off huge amounts of X-rays.

A New Observatory

In 1973, shortly after the Uhuru mission, Riccardo Giacconi and fellow scientists joined the newly formed Harvard-Smithsonian Center for Astrophysics (CfA) in Cambridge, Massachusetts. There, the team began designing and building an even larger and more powerful X-ray satellite. It was called an X-ray observatory. Scientists Harvey Tananbaum and Stephen Murray, who had helped design, build, and operate the earlier Uhuru satellite, were part of the team. So was scientist Leon Van Speybroeck.

The new X-ray observatory was a giant step forward from the Uhuru X-ray satellite. Unlike Uhuru, the observatory had an X-ray telescope along with new detectors and computers. It was named Einstein, after Albert Einstein.

Some telescopes that collect visible light use mirrors to collect and focus light. An X-ray telescope uses mirrors, too. But the mirrors in X-ray telescopes are shaped like cylinders. Einstein, with its X-ray telescope, was launched in 1978.

Above is a picture taken in visible light by the Very Large Telescope in Chile. It shows a supernova remnant called the Crab Nebula. Below is a picture made by the Einstein satellite. It shows X-rays given off by a supernova remnant in the Cygnus constellation.

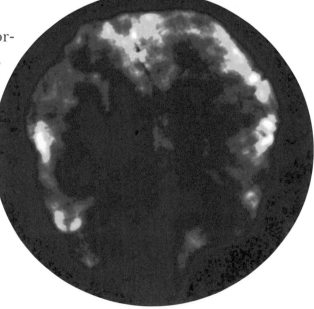

Looking into Space

Optical Telescopes

Optical telescopes collect visible light. In one kind of optical telescope, called a reflecting telescope, light enters a tube at one end and travels to a mirror at the other end. That mirror is shaped like a parabola. A parabola has a special property. It can focus light to a point. In this case, light that travels parallel to the sides of the telescope's tube is reflected by the parabolic mirror to a single point called the focus. (See the picture at right.)

Before the light reaches the focus, it strikes a flat mirror, placed at an angle. From there, the light is reflected again, to a hole on the telescope's side. An observer looks in this hole through an eyepiece. The eyepiece magnifies the image, making it appear larger.

X-ray Telescopes

X-ray telescopes are not designed in the same way as optical telescopes. As Leon Van Speybroeck explains, each X-ray particle has "so much energy that if it were to slam into a normal mirror head on, it would pass right through the surface and be absorbed by the mirror."

If X-rays hit a mirror at a very shallow angle, however, they "bounce," like stones skipping across a pond. So for an X-ray telescope, it is necessary to use mirrors that are cylinder-shaped. X-rays skim the mirror surfaces and come to a focus at the back of the telescope.

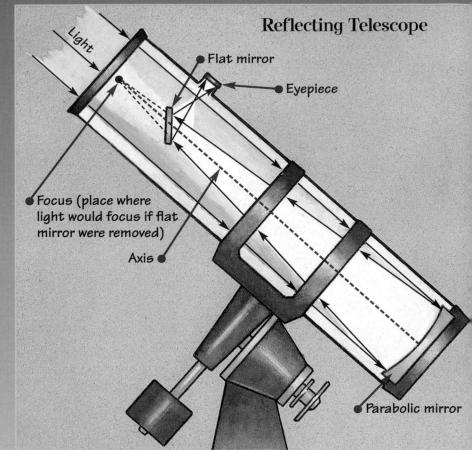

Reflecting Telescope

Light

Flat mirror

Eyepiece

Focus (place where light would focus if flat mirror were removed)

Axis

Parabolic mirror

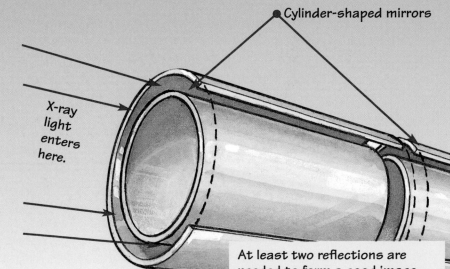

Cylinder-shaped mirrors

X-ray light enters here.

At least two reflections are needed to form a good image. With just one mirror, the image is blurry.

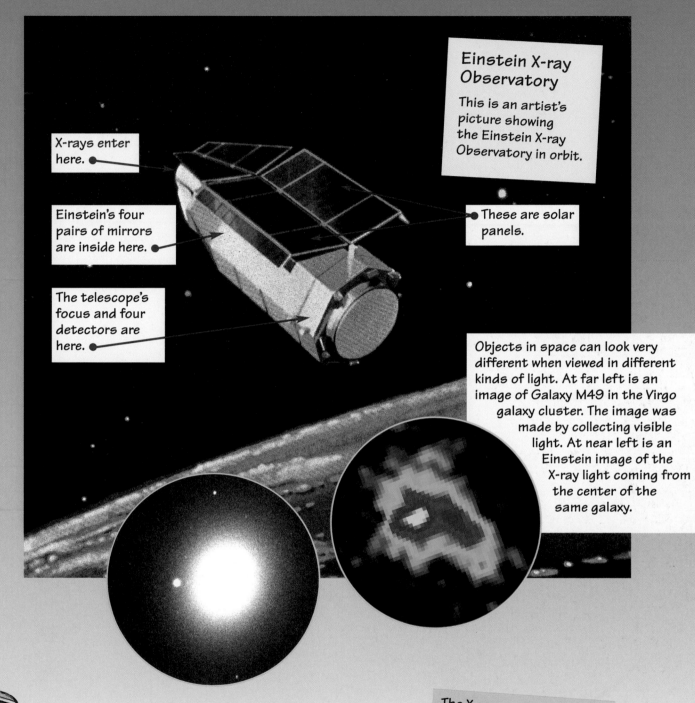

Einstein X-ray Observatory

This is an artist's picture showing the Einstein X-ray Observatory in orbit.

X-rays enter here.

Einstein's four pairs of mirrors are inside here.

The telescope's focus and four detectors are here.

These are solar panels.

Objects in space can look very different when viewed in different kinds of light. At far left is an image of Galaxy M49 in the Virgo galaxy cluster. The image was made by collecting visible light. At near left is an Einstein image of the X-ray light coming from the center of the same galaxy.

The X-rays meet at the focus where the detectors are placed. The detectors work like the observer's eyes at the eyepiece of an optical telescope. They record the X-rays.

Focus

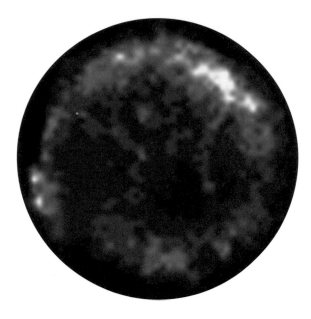

This is an image made by ROSAT. It shows the X-rays given off by the supernova remnant Tycho. The explosion of this Milky Way star was observed by Danish scientist Tycho Brahe in 1572.

New Eyes in Space

In more than two years of operation, Einstein located thousands of X-ray sources. It detected X-ray sources 1,000 times fainter than the ones Uhuru found. Einstein was also the first X-ray observatory that could take pictures showing the shape of X-ray sources other than the sun. Uhuru could only tell the direction in the sky from which the X-rays were coming.

In 1990 the German Space Agency launched a new X-ray observatory. The observatory was named the Röntgen Satellite, or ROSAT, after Wilhelm Röntgen, who discovered X-rays in 1895. Scientists learned much more about the X-ray universe during ROSAT's eight years of operation.

Uhuru, Einstein, and ROSAT made many discoveries. And they are just some of the X-ray telescopes that have scanned the sky. But scientists knew they could see more if they had better X-ray telescopes. The telescopes on Einstein and ROSAT weren't nearly as good at collecting X-rays as optical telescopes were at collecting visible light. A better observatory would help provide information that could help scientists solve more X-ray puzzles like Scorpius X-1 and Cygnus X-1. It could offer the chance to get clearer, more detailed images, or pictures, of X-ray sources. It could also allow them to observe dimmer X-ray sources.

It would take a lot of effort, and a lot of money, to make this dream come true. Making something new can be difficult. Scientists come up with a design of what they want to build, but they can't always follow the design exactly. Along the way there are problems to solve. Many things don't go right. But there can also be changes that make the design better. Scientists knew it would be a long road from the design to the finished observatory. But they were ready for the challenge.

This was the antenna for communicating with Earth.

These solar panels gathered sunlight to power the observatory.

ROSAT X-ray Telescope

ROSAT operated in orbit from 1990 until late 1998. It produced images from X-ray light. During its years of operation, it located 100,000 X-ray sources.

ROSAT's two detectors were located here.

ROSAT's mirrors were inside the observatory.

This ultraviolet camera helped aim the telescope. The job of all ROSAT's cameras was to make sure that ROSAT was aimed at the right object.

The wide-field telescope collected light for ultraviolet-light pictures.

The sunshield protected the telescope from the sun's rays.

X-rays entered ROSAT here.

This was an extra star camera.

The optical star camera helped ROSAT find the right object.

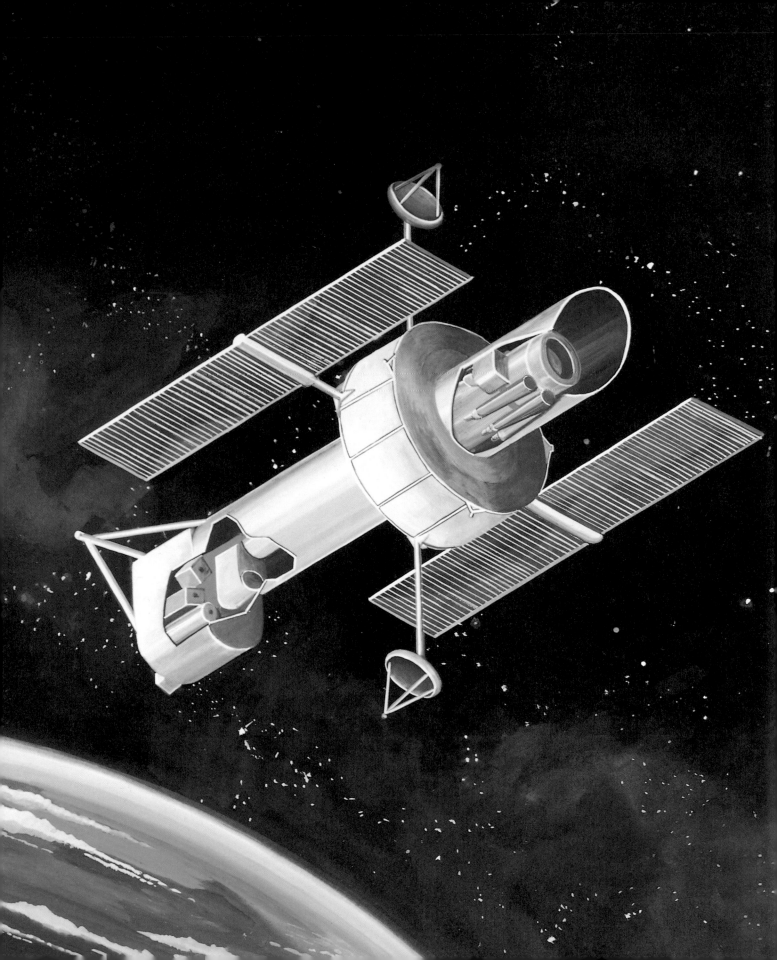

TRADE-OFFS

"We saved hundreds of millions of dollars. But there was a huge risk."—Martin Weisskopf

Even before Einstein launched, a team had formed to design a new X-ray observatory. The team included CfA scientists Harvey Tananbaum, Leon Van Speybroeck, and Stephen Murray. All of these people had worked on the Einstein observatory project. Martin Weisskopf, from NASA's Marshall Space Flight Center in Huntsville, Alabama, also joined the team. Harvey, Leon, Steve, and Martin planned the new observatory. At that time it was called the Advanced X-ray Astrophysics Facility, or AXAF.

AXAF was designed to have six pairs of cylinder-shaped mirrors. Each mirror was 80 centimeters (about 2½ feet) long. AXAF would also have four detectors. Something this large and with so many parts would be difficult to build. The mirrors would be the hardest of all. They needed to be much larger than any X-ray mirrors ever built. They also had to be incredibly smooth and perfectly shaped to focus the X-rays correctly. Meeting these requirements would be a big challenge.

In 1988 the United States Congress agreed to provide money for AXAF's design. But before paying to build it, Congress asked for a demonstration to show that the mirrors would work. Leon played an important role in designing the mirrors. "We had to prove that mirrors of the desired quality could be made," he says.

(above)
Harvey Tananbaum was a member of the planning group for AXAF. He holds an early model of the observatory.

(left)
This is an artist's picture of the original AXAF observatory. When it was first designed, AXAF included six pairs of mirrors and four detectors. As the amount of money for the project shrank, the design changed. Finally, four pairs of mirrors and two detectors were included in the design.

The AXAF team worked with the Perkin-Elmer Corporation in Danbury, Connecticut, to make two X-ray mirrors. The mirrors were finished in 1991. But did they have the right shape? Were they smooth enough? The pair of mirrors was shipped to the Marshall Space Flight Center, where a large building had been built just to test them. The mirrors passed all the tests.

But the amount of money for the project changed. In 1992 the U.S. Congress decided to reduce the amount of money it gave to many programs, including AXAF. The sum given to AXAF that year shrank from $211 million to $151 million.

The AXAF designers and engineers had to find a way to build an observatory for less money. First, they split

To prove the mirrors could work, two sample mirrors were made. One is shown below. The test mirrors were used in the finished observatory, though they had to be cut and polished further.

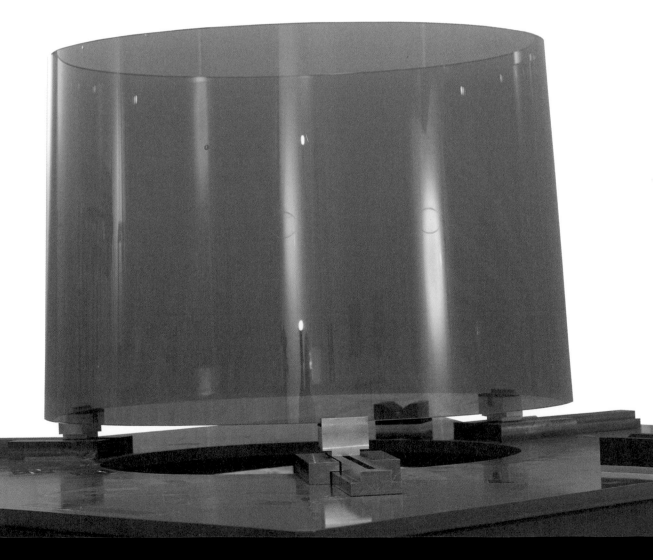

AXAF into two smaller observatories, AXAF-I and AXAF-S. AXAF-I would be used to take images of X-ray sources. It would then record their spectra, or the strength or brightness of the different X-rays these sources gave off. AXAF-S would also record the strength of different X-rays, but it would include much more detail.

The mirrors were tested at the Marshall Space Flight Center in Huntsville, Alabama.

Taking a Risk

Next, the team reduced the number of mirrors from six pairs to four, and the number of detectors from four to two. They also considered changing AXAF's orbit.

The team had first planned to put AXAF in a circular orbit around Earth only 400 kilometers (about 250 miles) above Earth's surface. They chose a low orbit because if something went wrong, a NASA Space Shuttle could reach the observatory, and astronauts could fix it. Also,

Martin Weisskopf was named the project scientist for AXAF. He would be responsible for making certain that the observatory met its scientific goals.

with AXAF so close to Earth, newer and better detectors and computers could be added. That way the observatory could be improved with time.

But it costs hundreds of millions of dollars to fly a Space Shuttle mission. And an observatory has to be built in a special way if it's going to be fixed in space. Building an observatory this way is very expensive, too.

The team could save a lot of money by building the observatory for a higher orbit. They wouldn't have to build it so astronauts could repair it. They wouldn't have to build new equipment to add to it. Nor would they need money to pay for repairs.

The AXAF team had a hard choice to make. They finally decided on a high elliptical, or oval-shaped, orbit. They weren't sure they had made the right decision. AXAF would have all kinds of machinery that could break. The astronauts wouldn't be able to reach it and make repairs. "We saved hundreds of millions of dollars," Martin says. "But there was a huge risk."

The high orbit also had advantages. The most important one was that AXAF would spend most of its time far from Earth. When a satellite is close to Earth, Earth blocks much of the satellite's view. A satellite far from Earth can receive data from almost every direction.

Putting the observatory in a high orbit had another advantage. Most planets, including Earth, have magnetic fields around them. Earth's magnetic field traps tiny, electrically charged particles. These particles stay in regions called radiation "belts," several thousand kilometers above Earth. Sometimes there are so many particles, they prevent a telescope's detectors from recognizing X-rays from space. But with the higher orbit, AXAF would spend most of its time above the radiation belts. "A five-year mission in high-Earth orbit is like a ten-year mission in low orbit. So that was a very good scientific trade," Martin explains. But, as Harvey said, "Everything had to work."

This picture shows the chosen AXAF orbit. The orbit reaches 140,000 kilometers (nearly 90,000 miles) above Earth at its farthest point. That's about one-third of the distance from Earth to the moon. The high, elliptical orbit lets the satellite spend most of its time far from Earth's radiation belts that would interfere with its ability to receive signals.

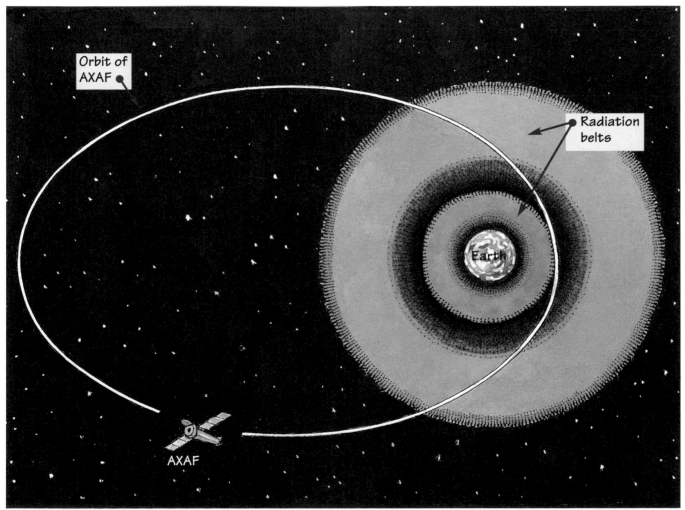

Orbit of AXAF

Radiation belts

Earth

AXAF

Satellite not to scale with its orbit and Earth

Sun is in this direction →

4

GETTING IT RIGHT

"We know we have the best X-ray mirrors ever made."—Harvey Tananbaum

The AXAF team members knew that building the observatory would be difficult. They had to bring together thousands of scientists, engineers, and other experts from all over the world. Everyone had to work together as a team to build a very complicated observatory.

Each NASA observatory is given a scientist's name at, just before, or just after launch. In December 1998 AXAF got a new name. It was called the Chandra X-ray Observatory (pronounced CHAN-drah), named for Indian-American physicist Subrahmanyan Chandrasekhar (soo-brah-MON-yon chan-drah-SAY-kar).

The Chandra X-ray Observatory was first designed with three major systems. These were the mirrors, the detectors, and the spacecraft. The mirrors would collect and focus X-rays from deep space. The detectors would record and analyze the X-rays. The spacecraft would perform tasks, such as providing electricity, recording data, and communicating with controllers. Controllers are people on the ground who are in charge of the observatory's activities. Of the three systems, the mirrors would be the greatest challenge.

(above)
Here is the arrangement of Chandra's four pairs of mirrors.

(left)
Chandra was the nickname of Subrahmanyan Chandrasekhar (1910–1995), shown at left in a photograph from the 1950s. He was one of the most brilliant scientists of his time.

27

The Chandra X-ray Observatory

This artist's picture of Chandra shows some of the observatory's main equipment.

Sunshade Door
The sunshade door works like the bill of a baseball cap to shade Chandra's mirrors from the sun's X-rays.

Aspect Camera
This camera helps controllers point Chandra in the desired direction.

Mirrors
Chandra holds four pairs of mirrors that together produce sharper images than those of any other X-ray observatory.

X-ray Light
X-ray light enters Chandra here.

Thrusters
The thrusters gently swing Chandra in a particular direction.

Insulation
Chandra is wrapped in insulation, or special material, to help keep a constant temperature inside.

Spacecraft Systems Equipment Compartment
This compartment holds Chandra's electronic equipment.

Detectors
The detectors record information that can be used to create an X-ray image and to study properties of an X-ray source, such as temperature.

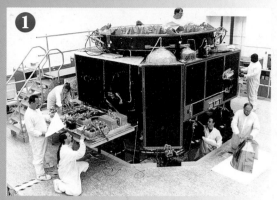
1

Thrusters

1 Spacecraft Systems Equipment Compartment

2 Mirrors

Telescope

This "exploded" view of Chandra shows how the three major systems of the observatory fit together. The thrusters, which are used to move Chandra, are also shown.

Detectors **3**

Chandra's equipment compartment is a huge container. The structure is almost 3 meters by 4 meters (10 feet by 13 feet). It is made of a special graphite-based material that is both lightweight and strong. Because Chandra is lightweight, it is cheaper to launch. And unlike many materials, graphite isn't strongly affected by temperature changes. It doesn't expand much when heated or contract much when cooled.

Solar Arrays
The two arrays provide about two kilowatts of power, the amount needed to run a hair dryer. But it's enough to run all of Chandra's computers, instruments, and communications systems.

Chandra's outermost mirrors are 120 centimeters (about 4 feet) across. The innermost mirrors are about 60 centimeters (about 2 feet) across. All of Chandra's mirrors are about 80 centimeters (about 2 1/2 feet) long. Together the mirrors weigh slightly more than one ton.

2

3

Chandra holds four instruments to capture the X-rays reflected by its mirrors—two detectors and two gratings. The detectors provide information about the X-rays, such as their number, position, and time of arrival. The gratings can be used to redirect incoming X-rays according to their wavelengths or energies. This separation allows the detectors, like the one shown at left, to measure the exact wavelengths or energies of the X-rays.

Making the Mirrors

The mirrors had to be almost perfect in shape, and the smoothest ever made. Sample mirrors had been made successfully. Now the real mirrors had to be built just as perfectly.

The mirrors started as cylinder-shaped slabs of amber-colored glass called Zerodur. Zerodur was chosen because it doesn't expand or contract very much when its temperature changes. This characteristic is important. A mirror that changes size too much can't reflect X-rays to exactly the same spot, or focus, every time. And if the X-rays aren't reflected to the same spot, the pictures won't be sharp enough. Because Zerodur was less sensitive to temperature changes, a simple temperature control system could keep the temperature of the mirrors almost constant. This control would help keep a perfect focus.

Chandra's four pairs of mirrors were sent to Hughes-Danbury Optical Systems in Danbury, Connecticut. This company used to be Perkin-Elmer, which made the test mirrors. There, the mirrors were shaped and polished. Engineers spent months using large machines to grind them to the correct shape. The engineers checked and rechecked the mirrors. They chose different polishing tools and methods to make a "polishing run" to correct any errors they found. Polishing runs and mirror checking were repeated until the mirrors were finished.

About 250 people worked on the project. The polishing machines ran day and night. Work went on around the clock. Because no one knew how many polishing runs would be needed, no one knew how long completing the work on the mirrors would take. "We worked 7 days a week, 24 hours a day. We had conference calls at

A small tool called a lap was used to grind the mirrors. As a machine turned each mirror, the lap slightly stroked the mirror. A tiny layer of glass came off with each stroke.

Approaching Perfection

1

Here, the first mirror that has been ground and polished is being inspected. It is one of the largest mirrors.

2

Here, one of the smallest mirrors undergoes its final inspection.

3

With the inspection of this last mirror, grinding and polishing of the mirrors are complete. Next, the mirrors will be coated with metal. Once the mirrors are coated with metal, they look much more like regular mirrors.

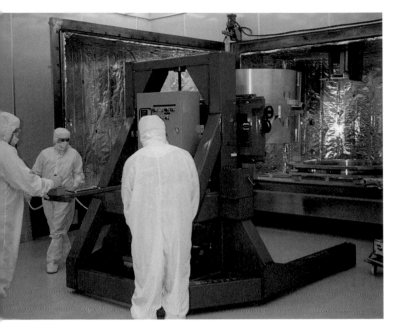

This picture shows the iridium coating being applied to a mirror inside a special coating chamber. The coating was only a few millionths of a centimeter thick. But it greatly increased the mirror's reflecting ability.

two in the morning," scientist Paul Reid of Hughes-Danbury remembers. But the work paid off. "We have the finest X-ray mirrors ever made, and they're also the largest," Paul says. In January 1995 the job was finished.

After manufacturing, the mirrors went to the Optical Coating Laboratory in Santa Rosa, California. There they would be coated with a rare metal called iridium. Iridium is very good at reflecting X-rays.

Once the mirrors were coated, they were shipped to the Eastman Kodak Company in Rochester, New York. The mirrors were then positioned, or mounted, together in the frame that would carry them to orbit. This operation and the tests to measure the mirrors' positions took place in a tall steel tower. If the mirrors were all going to reflect X-rays to the same focus point for the detectors, they had to be placed exactly right. "It's an incredibly difficult engineering feat," Harvey Tananbaum says.

Solving a Mystery

When work at Kodak was about half done, the engineers discovered a problem. Some of the tests showed that the mirrors were in the wrong positions. The error was small, but it was still a mystery.

The mirrors were inside a six-story tower. To keep dust away from them, the room was kept even cleaner than a hospital operating room. The temperature in the room was held constant to a few tenths of one degree Celsius. That way temperature changes wouldn't affect test results. The measuring system was so sensitive it could detect the temperature changes caused by people walking in and out of the tower.

Earlier tests had shown that the mirrors were positioned perfectly. The mirrors had not been moved. So

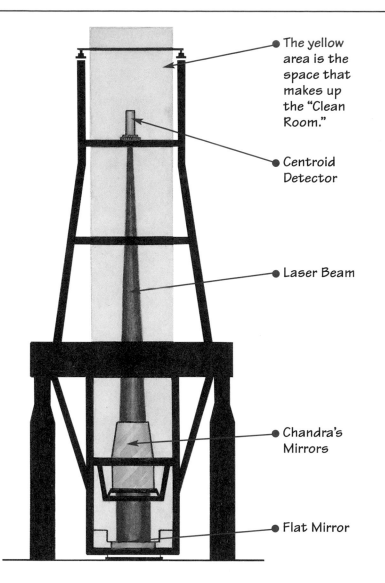

The yellow area is the space that makes up the "Clean Room."

Centroid Detector

Laser Beam

Chandra's Mirrors

Flat Mirror

Test Tower

An 18-meter (about 60-foot) test tower was used to check the position of Chandra's mirrors. For the test, a laser beam was sent from a device called a centroid detector. The detector was placed at the focal point for Chandra's mirrors.

The laser beam passed through Chandra's mirrors. It bounced off a flat mirror at the bottom of the tower and traveled back up through Chandra's mirrors to reach the centroid detector. The detector measured where the reflected light hit. The results would tell scientists whether Chandra's mirrors were in the correct positions.

what was wrong? The Kodak team checked the mirrors. They checked the test equipment. They checked the temperature controls. "We worked on it, worked on it, worked on it, but couldn't figure it out," Kodak chief engineer Gary Matthews remembers.

Gary and his team finally solved the problem. They realized that on the day they had bad test results, they hadn't turned on a set of lights at the top of the tower. They ran the test again with the lights off. The mirrors' positions still seemed to be slightly wrong. When they turned the lights back on, the positions were right.

"They were standard 40-watt fluorescent bulbs that you'd have in your home," Gary says. "There's nothing special about them." With the lights off, the temperature in the middle of the tower was about 0.03°C (about 0.05°F) cooler than the temperature at the outer edge of the tower. This temperature difference was enough to affect the tests. The tests should never have been done with the lights on.

Twenty light bulbs cost about $50. But these bulbs had caused a big problem in a billion-dollar project that involved many scientists and engineers. Often, even the smallest details can be very important.

NASA's Four Great Observatories

The Chandra X-ray Observatory is the third of NASA's four Great Observatories. These large space observatories are designed to detect light at different wavelengths.

The Hubble Space Telescope

The Hubble Space Telescope is the first of the four Great Observatories. Launched in 1990, Hubble collects mostly visible light. This picture is of the Ring Nebula, a ring of gas and material around a dying star. It was taken by one of Hubble's cameras.

The Compton Gamma-ray Observatory

The second Great Observatory was the Compton Gamma-ray Observatory, in operation from 1991 to 2000. It studied the universe in gamma rays. Compton detected gamma rays for this image of a solar flare, an explosion of gas on the surface of the sun.

The problem was corrected, and the mirrors were lined up properly. The mirrors next traveled to NASA's Marshall Space Flight Center. They were tested and retested. The mirrors had to be nearly perfect. And they were. "Because of the testing, we know we have the best X-ray mirrors ever made," Harvey says.

Chandra's mirrors focus X-rays to a point with a radius of less than three-hundredths of a millimeter. Chandra can see 10 to 50 times finer detail than any X-ray telescope used before. It is the first X-ray telescope to see as sharply as the best optical telescopes on the ground. Chandra's mirrors are making it possible for scientists to make big improvements in X-ray astronomy.

The Space Infrared Telescope Facility

The fourth of the Great Observatories is still being built. For now it is called the Space Infrared Telescope Facility (SIRTF). SIRTF will collect infrared light. Above is an example of the type of pictures SIRTF will make. This picture is of a supernova remnant called the Cygnus Loop. The image was made by a past infrared observatory. SIRTF is scheduled for launch in late 2001.

The Chandra X-ray Observatory

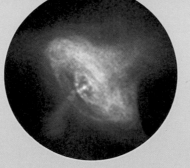

The Chandra X-ray Observatory detects X-ray light. Chandra took this image of a tiny part of the center of a supernova remnant. This remnant is called the Crab Nebula.

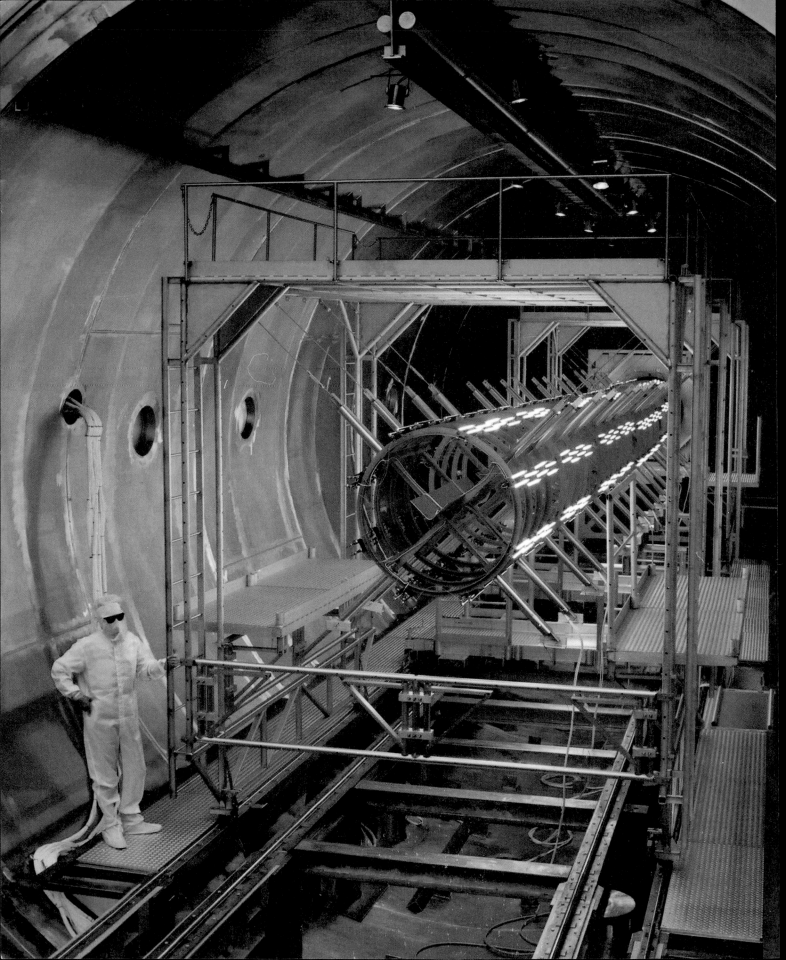

5

A BETTER IDEA

*"At the end of all this, the data is going to flow back. I'll be able to look at it
and either understand something I didn't understand before
or discover something I haven't seen before."—Steve Murray*

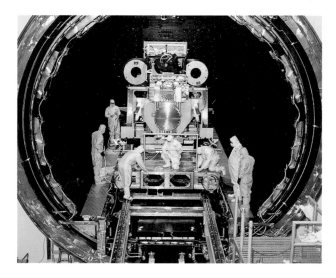

No matter how good Chandra's mirrors are, the observatory is only as good as its detectors. Just as the mirrors act like a camera's lens, the two detectors act like film. They record X-rays that bounce off the mirrors. Scientists also use two devices called gratings. Each grating is made of very fine gold wires. The wires are strung parallel to one another and are evenly spaced between frames. These gratings separate X-rays by their wavelengths, or energies. This information provides important clues about X-ray sources.

Chandra's two detectors are about 10 meters (33 feet) from the mirrors. The detectors are the High Resolution Camera (HRC) and the Advanced Charge-coupled device Imaging Spectrometer (ACIS). They work in very different ways. Together they provide more complete information about an energy source.

Steve Murray is an astrophysicist. A physicist often uses mathematics to make models of the natural world. An astrophysicist is a physicist who makes models of the natural world of outer space. But Steve is different from most astrophysicists. Most scientists don't have the time, energy, or skills to build the instruments that they use to find out about nature's behavior. For this, they rely on engineers.

(above)
Here, the HRC detector is being installed onto the mirror assembly in a test chamber at Marshall Space Flight Center. To test the HRC, X-rays will be focused onto the HRC from a distant source.

(left)
Because Chandra's systems are very sensitive to dust and oily film, testing areas are cleaned very carefully. Before it is used, the testing chamber is fitted with ultraviolet lamps. Heat from the lamps helps remove any fine dust or oil on the chamber walls. Here, the lamps are given a last check.

Calibration

This is astrophysicist Kathryn Flanagan. She was one of the team members whose job was to calibrate, or check and fix, all of Chandra's instruments. "You need to calibrate the instruments to understand how each one will perform," Kathryn says.

Each instrument was calibrated separately in the laboratory. The instruments were then shipped to the Marshall Space Flight Center to be calibrated together.

Steve is both a leading astrophysicist and a top instrument developer. He is an expert on supernova remnants and on galaxy clusters, groups of hundreds to thousands of galaxies. But Steve also designed Chandra's HRC and led the team that built it. He wanted the HRC to be better than past detectors.

Steve enjoys building instruments. He feels great satisfaction when everything works. Steve and a team of scientists and engineers worked on the HRC for more than 20 years. They sometimes worked 20 hours each day. "I think of myself as a scientist first and an instrument developer second," he says. "However, I spend more of my time developing instruments than doing astronomy."

Creative Solutions

Steve and his team came up with new ideas for the design of Chandra's HRC. It is much bigger than the detectors that were sent into orbit with Einstein in 1978 and with ROSAT in 1990. The HRC is 20 times larger than any earlier detector of its kind. It can also do more. It can collect more data, and higher quality data, than earlier detectors.

The HRC is made of 69 million glass tubes squeezed into a square called a microchannel plate. The plate is just 10 centimeters (4 inches) long on each side. The tiny tubes are each just one-eighth the thickness of a human hair and 1.2 millimeters (0.05 inches) long.

There is a special material on the surface of each tube. When an X-ray strikes one of the tubes, it knocks a tiny particle called an electron out of the material. As the electron moves down the tube, it bounces off the tube's wall, knocking off more electrons. Those electrons bounce against the tube's wall, too, releasing even more electrons. Eventually, several million electrons are released. Under the microchannel plate is a grid of electrically charged wires attached to a frame. The grid records the flood of electrons. Using this data, the detector can calculate the position and arrival time of the X-ray.

Steve's team thought that the HRC would work better if the microchannel plate were slightly curved to match the curve of the mirror. It was a good change to make, but the plates were too hard to bend. What was the team's solution? They used three plates. They put a flat plate in the middle and attached it to two plates that were turned upward.

That change solved one problem. But it created a new one. The wires behind the plates need to be very straight. It is also important that they always be at the same distance from the microchannel plate. Because the three plates now made a nonflat surface, wires that ran

Detectors

Door

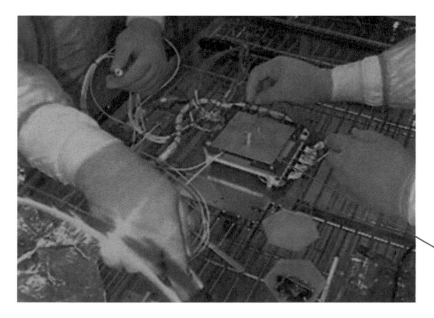

(above)
The HRC is made of two detectors. One detector makes images of X-rays, and the other detector records spectra. The HRC can be used over large areas. That makes it useful for making images of large objects.

(below)
Here, engineer Gerry Austin (left) and Steve Murray are finishing putting together a part of the HRC.

This is the microchannel plate.

Gratings of Gold

Hundreds of gold gratings can be placed between the mirrors and the detectors. These gratings change the direction of incoming X-rays according to their energies. This arrangement of X-rays is called a spectrum.

The strengths of the X-rays that appear at the different wavelengths or energies in this spectrum are characteristic of the particular elements that gave off the X-rays. From these X-ray "fingerprints," scientists can determine which elements are present and other information, such as their temperature.

Here, one of the grating instruments is being attached to the mirror assembly. The gratings, like the detectors, were calibrated separately. Then, they were put with the mirrors and detectors for further calibration. There were months of testing. Kathryn Flanagan remembers, "The instruments were tested in every possible way—mirrors alone, then mirrors and detectors together, then mirrors and gratings and detectors together."

along the curved side of the plates touched the plates. Wires that touched the microchannel plates would cause an electrical problem.

Steve's team thought they could solve this problem if they painted "ribbons" of gold on the frame under the plate. The ribbons would be parallel lines of gold paint, which could conduct electricity. These ribbons weren't real wires, but the team hoped they would act like wires.

The team wasn't sure their solution would work. They spent more than a year finding the right material and the right company to do the job. The effort was worth it.

The ribbons worked. "A lot of different areas of engineering and science had to come together to help us take a simple idea and turn it into something that could solve the problem," Steve says.

Working Together

Chandra's second detector, ACIS, was built by another team. The team's leader was scientist Gordon Garmire of Pennsylvania State University in University Park, Pennsylvania. He worked with a team from the Massachusetts Institute of Technology in Cambridge, Massachusetts. ACIS uses the same technology as a video camcorder. It contains an array, or arrangement, of detectors called charge-coupled devices (CCDs). A CCD is divided into individual cells like tiny buckets. Each cell collects X-rays that bounce down the mirrors. A CCD is laid out like a grid. Each bucket has its own position in the grid. This arrangement allows the detector to know where X-rays hit. The detector then creates a digital picture. ACIS's CCD array contains more than 1 million such cells. With a CCD array, ACIS would record each X-ray and measure the X-ray's energy.

The HRC is better for detecting wide objects, faint X-ray sources, and lower-energy X-rays. It does a better job of recording the arrival time of each X-ray. ACIS is better at determining the energy of individual X-rays. It can also detect higher-energy X-rays, that is, X-rays with shorter wavelengths. Which detector scientists use depends on what they want to learn.

A lot of hard work and clever thinking went into the development of both detectors. With the detectors in place, Chandra would soon be ready to see the X-ray universe.

Open and Shut

During the vacuum testing, a door to the ACIS instrument stuck shut. Team members spent several weeks trying to find the cause of the problem. Engineers thought a thin layer of ice might have caused the door to stick. They tried warming the detector, and it worked. But from then on, in test after test, the door always opened, even without being warmed.

"It shows that in spite of your best efforts, sometimes you never find out the real cause of a problem," says Scott Texter, a physicist on the ACIS team. "It also shows that by using good judgment, you can still solve a problem."

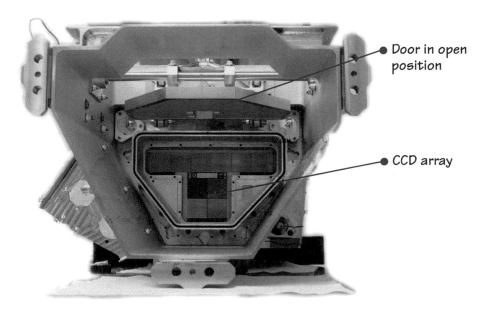

Door in open position

CCD array

6

TESTS, TESTS, AND MORE TESTS

"We exposed the spacecraft to the same level of sound energy it would experience during launch. Noise can make things rattle around, fall apart, and break. We wanted to make sure that wouldn't happen."—Scott Texter

The third major system in the Chandra X-ray Observatory was the spacecraft itself. It was put together by a company called TRW in Redondo Beach, California. The TRW company took parts of everything from computers to rocket engines to make the spacecraft. Then, TRW added the finished mirrors, detectors, and all the other parts of Chandra.

The whole observatory was wrapped in a material to insulate the inside from temperature changes outside. When everything was finally put together, the spacecraft was about the size of a large moving van.

Again it was time for more tests. TRW needed to make sure everything would work in the harsh conditions of space. Engineers left Chandra in a vacuum chamber, a room almost completely without air and dust, for 40 days. They exposed the observatory to temperatures as cold as -179°C (-290°F) to make sure it could withstand the extreme cold of space. The TRW team also made sure the spacecraft could communicate with Earth.

(above)
About 450 people at TRW worked to build and test Chandra. Here, technicians prepare for a series of tests on the strength of the spacecraft's main structure.

(left)
Technicians check the spacecraft's power supply and electrical systems as it is built. The power supply and electrical systems will be placed inside the spacecraft's main structure, which can be seen in the background.

43

Here, Chandra has just been lowered from the vacuum chamber at TRW after a month of testing at extreme temperatures. It passed all the tests. The silver-colored material around the observatory is the insulation.

Chandra would be separated from a Space Shuttle and then sent farther into space using its own rockets. The team wanted to be very certain that Chandra could survive the noise and vibration caused by the Space Shuttle's launch. Engineers came up with a way to test for this survival.

"We put the whole observatory in a large room with enormous speakers like the ones rock groups use," TRW physicist Scott Texter explains. "We exposed the spacecraft to the same level of sound energy it would experience during launch. Noise can make things rattle around, fall apart, and break. We wanted to make sure that wouldn't happen."

Technicians at TRW inspect Chandra's solar panels before the panels are added to the observatory.

Testing was finished in January 1999. Chandra was placed in a three-layer plastic bag for protection. Then, it was flown to the Kennedy Space Center at Cape Canaveral, Florida. In June 1999 NASA technicians attached a rocket called the Inertial Upper Stage (IUS) to Chandra. After Chandra's launch from the Space Shuttle, the IUS would power the observatory into the desired orbit.

Now complete, Chandra and its spacecraft weighed 22,750 kilograms (50,150 pounds). It was the heaviest and largest instrument ever launched by a Space Shuttle.

Clouds and smoke billow up into the sky as Space Shuttle Columbia lifts off.

This photograph of (from left) mission specialist Steve Hawley, commander Eileen Collins, pilot Jeff Ashby, and mission specialists Michel Tognini and Cady Coleman was taken during the flight.

One Minute and Counting

July 20, 1999, was launch day. Chandra waited in the Space Shuttle Columbia. Eileen Collins, the first woman to command an American space mission, was in charge of the flight. Three mission specialists, or people given special jobs to perform, were on board Columbia. They were responsible for sending Chandra towards its orbit.

NASA started the countdown. One minute and counting...30 seconds and counting...10...9...8...7... With 7 seconds to go, the countdown stopped. A computer had detected a dangerous level of gases in one of Columbia's engines. The launch would have to wait for another day.

Engineers later realized that nothing was wrong. Columbia could have taken off safely. But NASA wasn't taking any chances. Columbia finally launched at 12:31 A.M. on July 23. During launch, something did go wrong. Gas began to leak from one of Columbia's engines. Because of the leak and a minor electrical problem, the Space Shuttle was carried about 5 kilometers (3 miles) short of NASA's planned 283-kilometer (176-mile) altitude orbit. Eileen had to fire small rocket engines called thrusters to reach the proper altitude. But the problems didn't threaten the crew's safety.

Shortly after Columbia entered orbit, the crew prepared Chandra for launch. They turned on Chandra's power and communications systems. Next, they tilted the platform to which Chandra and the IUS were attached. Two hours later the crew set off small explosive charges to cut the bolts that kept Chandra and the IUS attached to Columbia. Then, six powerful coiled springs that had been attached to Columbia were released. The springs pushed Chandra and the IUS slowly away from the Space Shuttle.

After a few moments, Eileen fired small rockets from the front of Columbia to move the Space Shuttle away from Chandra. Fifteen minutes later, she fired the rockets again, and Columbia moved farther away. The crew then fired the IUS, sending the observatory toward its orbit. Chandra's thrusters later fired several times to put the observatory in the correct orbit.

So far, so good. Chandra was orbiting Earth in the correct path. And on the night of July 27, Columbia's crew landed safely at Kennedy Space Center. The Chandra team was excited, but nervous. Chandra was where it was supposed to be. But would everything work?

Assistant flight director Gwen Artis (from right), flight directors Lewis Wooten and Steve Terry of NASA's Marshall Space Flight Center, and operations controller Chuck Smith of TRW celebrate. The liftoff of Space Shuttle Columbia, which carried the Chandra X-ray Observatory, was successful.

7

FINAL EXAMS

"Testing the observatory's systems is like learning to drive a car, except the observatory is a much, much more complicated vehicle."—Harvey Tananbaum

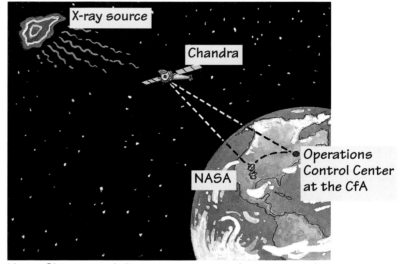

Note: Objects and distances are not drawn to scale.

Chandra wouldn't be very useful if it couldn't communicate with Earth. Scientists need to tell Chandra when and where to point in space. They also have to tell Chandra to fire its thrusters from time to time to adjust its pointing direction. And Chandra needs to send its pictures and data back to Earth. It also needs to update the controllers on the "health" of its systems.

The ground team communicates with the Chandra observatory through the Operations Control Center, located in Cambridge, Massachusetts. About 50 people work at the Operations Control Center. Flight director Roger Brissenden of the CfA is the head of this team.

Roger and his team communicate with Chandra using a network of NASA radio antennae, called the Deep Space Network. Some of the antennae are located in Spain, some in Australia, and some in California. They are in different parts of the world so that as Earth rotates, at least one of the antennae will always be in contact with Chandra. NASA's Jet Propulsion Laboratory, in Pasadena, California, sends signals back and forth between the Deep Space Network and the Operations Control Center.

(above)
Chandra's data are sent from the observatory to NASA's Deep Space Network receiver. The receiver sends the data to the Operations Control Center. Data include observations of X-ray sources, information on how much power Chandra uses, Chandra's temperature, and other important information.

(left)
This is an artist's picture of Chandra in the bay of the shuttle Columbia, ready to be sent towards its final orbit. At almost 14 meters (about 46 feet), Chandra is the largest satellite the Space Shuttle has ever placed in space.

49

Scientist Jonathan McDowell (below) is part of the team that helps calibrate Chandra's instruments. He will also be using Chandra to observe and record the X-rays given off by M33, a nearby galaxy. Jonathan says he "wants to understand the big picture of a galaxy in X-rays." The X-rays from M33 (above) can give scientists more detailed information because M33 is closer to Earth than most galaxies. This information will help scientists describe a "typical galaxy." This description can then be compared with observations of more distant galaxies.

Many different spacecraft also need to use the Deep Space Network. So Chandra's flight controllers can only communicate with the spacecraft every eight hours. Controllers "talk" to Chandra for about one hour at a time.

Each week the Operations Control Center sends Chandra a new set of instructions about where to point and when to take pictures and collect data. The commands are then stored in Chandra's computer and Chandra follows them during the week.

Chandra's data are sent to the Chandra X-ray Center, which is operated by the CfA. Researchers there change the data into computer files. Scientists on Chandra projects can study these files more easily. The scientists have one year to study the files before the data are put in a public library. This gives the researchers who set up the projects time to publish their results. Eventually all Chandra data will be available to everyone.

But there's not enough time for all the scientists who want to use Chandra. Who gets to use the observatory? The scientists who helped design and build Chandra received 30 percent of the first year's total observing time. Other scientists competed for the remaining time. They wrote proposals explaining what they wanted to observe, why, and how much time it would take. Only 200 of the 800 proposals that were written resulted in scientists being given observing time.

Planning Ahead

One of the Chandra X-ray Center's most important jobs is to plan Chandra's observing schedule. It takes time for Chandra to point itself at each target. Other activities also take time. To change detectors and gratings, for example, a command is sent from the ground to the computer on Chandra. The computer tells a device to put a grating in place, or to switch from one detector to another. It takes about three minutes to move a grating, and about five minutes to change detectors. Scientists want Chandra's schedule to allow them to observe as many targets as possible.

There are many things to consider in planning Chandra's activities. For example, Chandra's solar panels must always point toward the sun, but the telescope itself must not. The sun's intense X-rays would damage Chandra's equipment. So X-ray sources that lie close to the plane of Earth's orbit can only be observed during certain times of the year. The Chandra X-ray Center uses a computer to plan the best schedule. But, Roger says, "The computer may do something that a human can plainly see is not the [best] thing." When this happens, the Center changes the schedule.

Harvey Tananbaum is the director of the Chandra X-ray Center. He makes sure everything runs smoothly. He communicates with scientists, NASA, and the detector teams. He also has authority to change Chandra's observing plan if an unusual X-ray event happens. That is a lot of responsibility for just one person. But Harvey is up to these challenges.

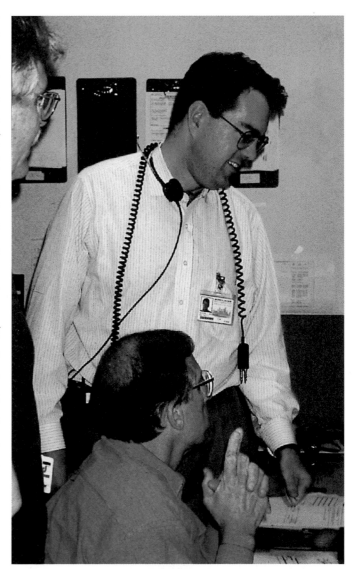

Roger Brissenden (standing) and Harvey Tananbaum (sitting) are in the Operations Control Center. They are receiving proof that Chandra has locked onto its First Light target. First Light is the moment when a telescope cover is opened and the telescope looks out into space for the first time. The telescope is usually aimed at a well-known object. That way scientists can compare the view through the new telescope with those from other, well-tested telescopes.

Point, Aim, and Click

To make an observation, Chandra uses a small optical telescope called an aspect camera. This camera helps Chandra's engineers point the satellite in the right direction. A computer in the camera contains the positions of several "guide stars." The computer uses the guide stars to help the camera find its targets.

Another system guides Chandra's telescope to help keep it locked on the target. Guiding Chandra is important. Observations of many X-ray sources require a long time. These sources give off relatively few X-rays in a given time.

The attempt to guide Chandra's telescope is only partly successful. The images of objects gathered from long observations look fuzzy because the telescope is moving. To help "defuzz" images, another camera is attached to Chandra. This camera takes a picture of where the telescope is pointing every second. The exact time each X-ray arrives is also recorded. All the pictures can then be combined to make one picture. This picture shows the images as they would appear if the telescope had stayed still during the total time observations were made.

The results are the sharpest X-ray images ever seen. Here are three of Chandra's first images.

This is a supernova remnant in a small galaxy. The remnant is about 1,000 years old. The circular shape is extremely hot, expanding gas. Chandra's ACIS detector was used to make this image.

Eta Carinae gives off more light than most of the stars known in our galaxy. Chandra's ACIS detector was used for this image.

N132D is the remnant of an exploded star. Scientists estimate that the remnant is about 3,000 years old. Chandra's HRC detector was used to make this image.

Test Drive

During the first two months Chandra was in space, the observatory's systems were tested. An Operations Control Center team checked each instrument and system. "It's like learning to drive a car," Harvey says, "except it's a much, much, more complicated vehicle." (And, of course, the "driver" is many thousands of kilometers away.)

Less than one month after Chandra was put in space, a command was sent to open its HRC door. The team was relieved when the detector passed all the tests.

The ACIS detector was next. It was this detector's door that had failed to open in a past test. The reason for the problem had never been found. Would it happen again? A command was sent to open the door. The team watched anxiously through two tries. Success came on a third try. The command got through and the door opened. ACIS was ready for testing.

On August 12, another command was sent to Chandra. The command told Chandra to use an explosive charge to send a chisel through a bolt. That caused a powerful spring to push open a 54-kilogram (120-pound) door. The door to Chandra's mirrors was open!

Chandra's systems and equipment were ready to begin their work. The first images beamed back by Chandra showed supernova remnants and other X-ray sources in amazing detail. The years of hard work and attention were paying off.

Chandra Delivers

Astrophysicist Christine Jones uses Chandra to study elliptical galaxies. An elliptical galaxy appears as a nearly round cloud of stars. Before X-ray telescopes, scientists couldn't detect gas in elliptical galaxies. But it was there.

The temperature of the gas in elliptical galaxies is so high that the gas can't be seen in visible light. The gas gives off most of its light in X-rays. More massive elliptical galaxies hold on to this hot gas. But less massive galaxies probably can't.

Christine studies different elliptical galaxies to find out how much mass is needed to hold the gas. She also tries to find out how the spectra, or strengths of the X-rays at different wavelengths or energies, vary from galaxy to galaxy. Chandra is now observing several galaxies, including Centaurus A. An X-ray image of Centaurus A is shown on the screen beside Christine.

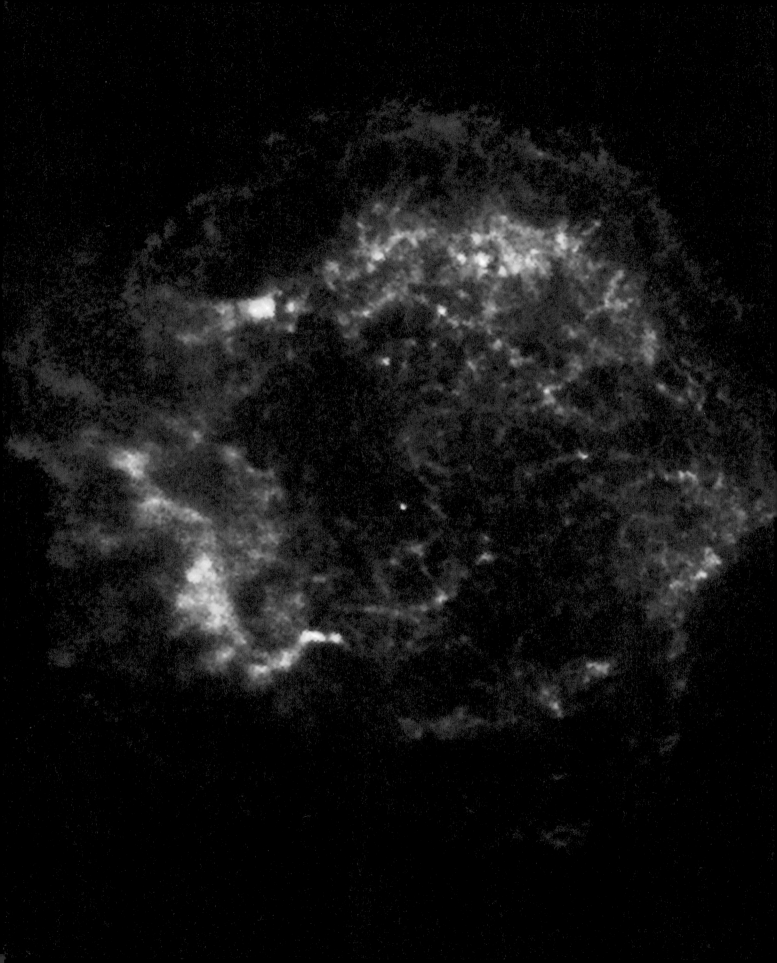

8

A DREAM COME TRUE

"Getting the first pictures back from Chandra was one of the top ten moments of my life."—Steve Murray

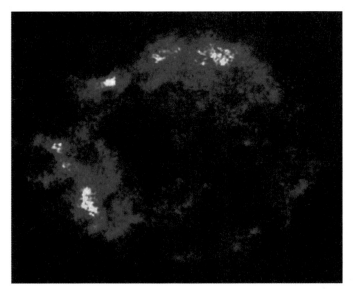

In September 1999 testing came to an end and Chandra began normal scientific observations. The first picture Chandra sent back to Earth was an ACIS image of a supernova remnant called Cassiopeia A, or Cas A. It is the closest supernova remnant to Earth. Chandra's image of Cas A showed much greater detail than any of the earlier X-ray images. It took more than 90 minutes to collect the data to make this image.

The first images thrilled and relieved the thousands of people who worked on Chandra. "The launch was exciting," Steve Murray says. "But even more exciting was going back to the Operations Control Center, turning the detector on, and seeing it come to life."

Unfortunately, while ACIS's door was open for First Light, Chandra was passing through Earth's radiation belt. Electrically charged particles damaged the ACIS detector slightly. But the HRC detector was working well. It could provide scientists with most of the data they needed. "Even if something were wrong with the ACIS detector, all of Chandra's science goals would be met," Roger Brissenden says.

The image also brought a major surprise. There was

(above)
Cassiopeia A is the remnant of a star that exploded about 300 years ago. The X-ray image shows an expanding shell of super-hot gas. This image of Cassiopeia A was taken by ROSAT.

(left)
This is an image of Cassiopeia A taken by the Chandra X-ray Observatory. The Chandra image has much more detail than the ROSAT image. It even shows a small, bright dot almost in the center of the remnant. This dot probably shows the presence of a neutron star created during the supernova explosion.

From left, scientists Mark Bautz, Martin Weisskopf, Beverly Ferguson LaMarr, Gordon Garmire, and Hank Donnelly receive some of Chandra's early images at the Chandra X-ray Center. Gordon Garmire proposed and was responsible for delivering the ACIS detector, and Mark Bautz was responsible for building it.

a tiny, bright dot near the center of Cas A. Scientists thought that the explosion that created Cas A had left behind a neutron star. But they had never seen it. It will take more study to be sure the dot is a neutron star, but most scientists think it probably is.

Questions for Chandra

Scientists have many questions about the universe that Chandra can help answer. Roger would like to know how fast the material around black holes moves. Martin Weisskopf, who was part of the original team that designed Chandra, wants to know the surface temperature of neutron stars. Leon Van Speybroeck, another member of the original design team, wants to know how the amounts of the various chemical elements in galaxy clusters change over time. Leon will compare the amounts of chemical elements in galaxy clusters of different ages.

Steve would like to know if there are new kinds of X-ray sources that haven't been seen before. To answer this question, his team will point Chandra at a small part of space for four days. "One of the reasons I built the HRC was to make this observation," he says. "Using Chandra, we should be able to see objects 10 to 50 times fainter than what's already been found. The only way to find something new is to look hard."

Riccardo Giacconi, a member of the team who first found evidence of X-rays coming from outer space, will also be using Chandra. He is part of a group that will observe another small part of space for nearly six days. It's an area where there are no obvious X-ray sources.

Using Chandra's powerful mirrors and detectors, Riccardo and his team should be able to see very faint, very distant clusters of galaxies. By comparing distant clusters with nearby clusters, his team will learn more about how clusters are different from one another. This knowledge will help scientists develop a model of how the universe came to be the way it is today.

And there will be new mysteries for Chandra. "When you have a new telescope like Chandra, you will find new things," Harvey Tananbaum says. "Some of the most exciting questions are ones we haven't been able to ask yet. We haven't learned enough to ask them."

Mystery in the Making

The Andromeda Galaxy is the nearest large galaxy to the Milky Way. It's also the most studied galaxy, after our own. Data have indicated that there might be a very large black hole in the galaxy's center. Chandra's first X-ray picture (below) of Andromeda showed an X-ray source (shown in blue) at the center of the galaxy, just where the black hole ought to be.

Chandra's data also showed something different in the X-rays coming from gas moving toward the possible black hole. They were cooler than X-rays measured near other black holes. Scientists don't know yet why temperatures near this black hole would be different. It may mean scientists will need a new model of black hole behavior. And it's all because of Chandra's ability to make such clear pictures.

Steve Murray says that it's almost as if "previous X-ray images were taken with a slightly out-of-focus black-and-white camera, while the Chandra image is taken with a sharp, color camera. I expect that our future pictures will lead to more exciting discoveries in the Andromeda Galaxy."

X-ray Future

Scientists have another powerful X-ray observatory to help them study the universe. On December 10, 1999, the European Space Agency launched the X-ray Multiple-mirror Mission Newton Space Observatory (XMM-Newton).

On February 8, 2000, Japan's Institute of Space and Astronautical Science also launched an X-ray observatory, Astro-E. Unfortunately, the observatory was lost during launch. The rocket had a steering problem and Astro-E never made it to orbit. Instead, it burned up in the atmosphere. Astro-E was designed to add to Chandra and XMM-Newton's abilities. It would have measured spectra of very high-energy X-ray sources.

Chandra and XMM-Newton have different strengths and weaknesses. Chandra has the best mirrors, so it will take the sharpest pictures. XMM-Newton will collect the most light for detailed spectra.

The XMM-Newton has three pairs of mirrors and one small visible and ultraviolet light telescope. Its most important job is to collect very detailed spectra on X-ray sources.

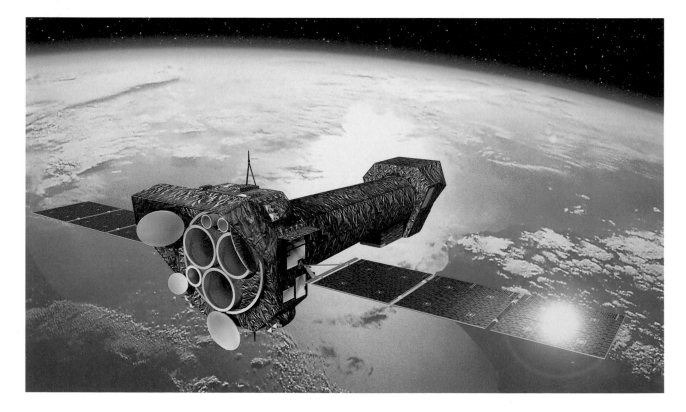

Nobody can tell exactly how long Chandra will operate. It has backup systems that should keep it working for at least five years, and probably much longer. But it won't last forever. About once an orbit, controllers order Chandra to fire its thrusters to keep it pointing in the desired direction. After about 10 or 15 years, Chandra will run out of fuel and the mission will end. But during those years of operation, Chandra will make discoveries that will change our understanding of the universe.

"We are grateful to the people of the United States for supporting this program," Leon says. "I hope we increase people's enjoyment of life by letting them know a little bit more about our wondrous universe."

Chandra's mission is just beginning. In the years ahead, Chandra's observations will provide new information and discoveries about the X-ray universe.

GLOSSARY

astrophysicists Physicists who study objects in space.

atmosphere Gases around a star or planet, such as Earth.

black hole A space object so dense that not even light can escape from it.

constellation A set of stars in the sky that forms a recognizable pattern in people's imaginations.

density The amount of matter in a specific amount of space.

detector A device that takes in light coming from an object.

electron A very tiny particle that carries an electric charge.

First Light The moment when a telescope cover is opened and the telescope looks out into space for the first time.

galaxy A collection of hundreds of billions of stars. Our sun and its planets are in the Milky Way galaxy.

galaxy cluster A group of galaxies.

gamma rays Light that we cannot see with our eyes. In the wave model of light, gamma rays have the shortest wavelengths.

grating A device placed in front of a detector. The grating separates light into its different wavelengths.

infrared light Light that we cannot see with our eyes. According to the wave model of light, infrared light has longer wavelengths than visible light.

launch To use a rocket to lift an object, such as a space shuttle, into outer space.

NASA (National Aeronautics and Space Administration) The United States' space agency. It sends spacecraft and crews into space to investigate Earth, the solar system, and the rest of the universe.

neutron star A dense object often produced after a star explodes. A neutron star is made mostly of neutrons.

observatory A place on the ground or in space that contains one or more telescopes.

optical telescope A telescope designed to detect and focus visible light.

orbit The path in space along which an object moves.

radio waves Light that we cannot see with our eyes. In the wave model of light, radio waves have longer wavelengths than infrared light.

satellite A natural or human-made object in space that moves in an orbit around a planet.

solar array A group of devices that collect sunlight. The collected sunlight is then used to produce electrical power.

spectrum A range of wavelengths of light. For light visible to human eyes, a spectrum is the range of colors from red to blue to violet that we see when sunlight passes through a prism.

supernova The explosion of a large star.

supernova remnant The expanding cloud of gas that comes from a supernova.

ultraviolet light Light that we cannot see with our eyes. According to the wave model of light, ultraviolet light has shorter wavelengths than visible light.

vacuum chamber A room from which almost all the air and dust have been removed.

visible light Light that we can see with our eyes.

wavelength The distance from any part of a wave to the same part of the next (or previous) wave.

X-ray telescope A telescope designed to detect and focus X-rays.

X-rays Light that we cannot see with our eyes. According to the wave model of light, X-rays have shorter wavelengths than ultraviolet light and longer wavelengths than gamma rays. According to the particle model of light, X-rays have more energy than ultraviolet light and less energy than gamma rays.

FURTHER READING

Beasant, Pam. *1000 Facts About Space.* New York, NY: Larousse Kingfisher Chambers, 1992.

Dickinson, Terence. *Exploring the Night Sky.* New York, NY: Firefly Books, 1988.

Ford, Harry. *The Young Astronomer.* New York, NY: Dorling Kindersley Publishing, 1998.

Miles, Lisa, and Alastair Smith. *The Usborne Complete Book of Astronomy and Space.* Tulsa, OK: EDC Publications, 1998.

National Wildlife Federation. *Astronomy Adventures.* Ranger Rick's Naturescope. New York, NY: Learning Triangle Press, 1997.

The New York Public Library. *The New York Public Library Amazing Space: A Book of Answers for Kids.* New York Public Library Answer Books for Kids. New York, NY: John Wiley & Sons, 1997.

Rey, H. A. *The Stars: A New Way to See Them.* Boston, MA: Houghton Mifflin, 1976.

Ridpath, Ian, et al. *Eyewitness Handbooks: Stars and Planets.* New York, NY: Dorling Kindersley Publishing, 1998.

VanCleave, Janice P. *Janice VanCleave's Astronomy for Every Kid: 101 Easy Experiments That Really Work.* New York, NY: John Wiley & Sons, 1991.

INDEX

Acknowledgments

We offer special thanks to Dr. Irwin Shapiro, Director of the Harvard-Smithsonian Center for Astrophysics, who took a particular interest in this series, and made time in a very crowded schedule to work closely with us to ensure the material's accuracy and completeness. Thanks also to Matt Schnepps, Tania Ruiz, Mark Waldman, and Surya Dill. The author wishes to gratefully acknowledge the help and support of the following people who were interviewed for this book: Roger Brissenden, Lester Cohen, Riccardo Giacconi, Gary Matthews, Brooks McKinney, Steve Murray, Paul Reid, Fred Seward, Harvey Tananbaum, Scott Texter, Wallace Tucker, Leon Van Speybroeck, Martin Weisskopf, and Donna Wyatt. The author would also like to thank Audrey Bryant, Bonnie Gordon, Ray Jayawardhana, Meg Kassakian, Susan Sherman, Richard Talcott, and Erica Thrall for their ongoing help and support.

Photographs courtesy of:

AURA/NOAO/NSF: 17 bottom left; Caltech/JPL: 35 top right; CfA: 7, 8, 12, 20, 26, 29 bottom, 38, 39 bottom, 41 bottom; Chase, Jon: 21, 50 bottom, 53; Compton Gamma-ray Observatory: 34 bottom right; European Southern Observatory (ESO): 15 top; European Space Agency: 58; Finley Holiday Film: 2 top left, 50 top; Fletcher, Bill and Sally: 14; The Francis A. Countway Library of Medicine, Boston, Massachusetts: 6; High Energy Astrophysics Science Archive Research Center (HEASARC)/NASA: 15 bottom, 17 bottom right, 17 main image; Infrared Processing and Analysis Center, Marshall Space Flight Center: 36, 37; Johnson Space Center: 34 top left; Kurita, Naoyuki: 5; Malin, David/Anglo-Australian Observatory: 8 right, 9 top; Marshall Space Flight Center: 23, 24; Max Planck Institute: 18, 19, 55; McDonald, Kim: 13 middle; NASA: 10, 13 bottom, 46, 48; NASA/CXC/SAO: cover background, 1 background, 2 middle, 3 top, 26, 34 top right, 35 bottom left, 51, 52, 54, 56, 57 inset, 59; NASA/D. Drachlis: 47; NASA/Hubble Space Telescope: 34 bottom right; Optical Coating Laboratory (OCL): 32; Raytheon Systems Company: 22, 29 middle, 30, 31; Smithsonian Astrophysical Observatory (SAO): 11; Space Infrared Telescope Facility: 35 bottom right; TRW, Inc.: cover inset, 1 inset, 2 right, 3 bottom, 28–29, 29 top, 35 top left, 40, 42, 43, 44, 45; Ware, Jason: 57 top; White Sands Missile Range: 4, 13 top.

Illustrations on pages: 16, 25, 29, 33, 39, and 49 are by Dave Griffin.

The illustration on page 27 is by Gregg Dinderman, courtesy of *Sky and Telescope*.